The Great Commission, According to Jesus

Six week study prior to Faith Promise Commitment Sunday

And the word of God increased...the number of
the disciples multiplied...greatly...Acts 6:7

Dr. James Wilkins

YAKIMA BIBLE BAPTIST CHURCH
6201 TIETON DRIVE
YAKIMA, WA. 98908
509-966-1912

The Great Commission, According to Jesus

Six week study prior to Faith Promise Commitment Sunday

And the word of God increased…the number of the disciples multiplied…greatly…Acts 6:7

Dr. James Wilkins

Copyright © 2011 New Testament Ministries. All rights reserved.

Writings contained herein are by the author unless otherwise stated.

No part of this publication may be reproduced, stored in a retrieval system or transmitted in any way by any means—electronic, mechanical, photocopy, recording or otherwise—without the prior permission of the copyright holder, except as provided by USA copyright law.

Printed in the United States of America.

All Scriptures are taken from the King James Bible.

ISBN # 978-1-61119-056-4

Printed by Calvary Publishing
A Ministry of Parker Memorial Baptist Church
1902 East Cavanaugh Road, Lansing, Michigan 48910
www.CalvaryPublishing.org

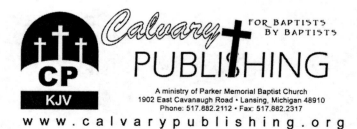

Table of Contents

Principle One   9
THE PROPER MOTIVE TO STUDY THE BIBLE

Principle Two   11
THE PROPER METHOD OF GROWING IN FAITH

Principle Three   13
THE PROPER METHOD IN DEVELOPING A GOOD PRAYER LIFE

Principle Four   15
THE PROPER METHOD OF RETAINING BIBLE TRUTH

Principle Five   17
IT CREATES THE PROPER METHOD OF CONTROLLING THE FLESH.

LESSON ONE   25
THE GREAT COMMISSION IN PROPORTION

LESSON TWO   41
THE GREAT COMMISSION AND ITS PERSONNEL

LESSON THREE   59
THE GREAT COMMISSION IN PERSPECTIVE

LESSON FOUR 75
THE GREAT COMMISSION IN PARTICULAR

LESSON FIVE 93
THE GREAT COMMISSION IN POWER

LESSON SIX 115
YOUR FINANCIAL OBLIGATION TO GIVE
UNDER THE GREAT COMMISSION

Foreword

The Great Commission According to Jesus is a book which features all the words of Jesus pertaining to his commission or **mandate to his church**. These words will be studied over a period of six-weeks and were written to be used the six weeks **prior to Faith Promise Commitment Sunday.**

If a person fully grasps the information contained in these lessons it will cause him to become a much better and obedient Christian. It is for this reason the author reverted back to when he became a Christian over 60 years ago. He re-introduces the method and philosophy which were used in some churches back then, He calls this method of Bible study **"The Study-to-Learn-and-Do Method."**

In order **to obtain the best results** from this series of studies the author recommends the books be passed out to the class **the Sunday before** the six-week study on the Great Commission begins. Use that Sunday to review the Study-to-Learn-and-Do Method in front of the book and the grading system.

WORD OF GOD INCREASES…REVIVAL FOLLOWS

Throughout man's history when the words of the Bible were studied and obeyed great revival followed.

In the days of Nehemiah the people stood as the Word of God was read to them. The people then signed a pact or covenant that they would observe to do God's words (Nehemiah 10:29) **A Great revival followed.**

In Josiah's day they found the lost law. It was read and obeyed. In the darkest period of Israel's history, a sweeping revival followed.

The secret of the great revival which started in Jerusalem and swept across the world is stated in Acts 6:7 **"And the word of God increased; and the number of the disciples multiplied in Jerusalem greatly;..."**

The Word of God works – if only we can get people to understand and do it.

We believe this Study-to-Learn-and-Do Method has a better chance of getting our people to work than what most churches are doing today.

WELCOME TO OUR STUDY
Introduction:

Principle One

THE PROPER MOTIVE TO STUDY THE BIBLE

Of these things put them in remembrance, **charging them before** the Lord that they strive not about words to no profit, **but to the subverting** of the hearers. **Study** to shew thyself approved unto God, **a workman** that needeth not to be ashamed, rightly dividing the word of truth.
                    II Timothy 2:14:15

> In verse 15 the Child of God is commanded to **study** the Bible.
> It is **not** a command to read the Scriptures, **but study**
> It is **not** a command to listen to the Scriptures, **but study**
> It is **not** a command to discuss the Scriptures, **but study**

NOTICE THE CLEAR COMMAND
It is to study in order to become a **WORKMAN**, who will not be ashamed when he stands before God.
  Please take note:
>   It is not to become a **Student** of the Word
>   It is not to become a **Discusser** of the Word
>   It is not to become a **Teacher** of the Word

We are to study in order to become a **Doer** of the Word - a **Workman - Doer - Performer**.

II Timothy 2:14 should be read and become familiar

to the Child of God, as should II Timothy 2:15. In verse 14, Paul tells the young workman, Timothy, "Of these things put them into remembrance, **charging them before the Lord** [Boss] that they strive not about **Words** to no profit, but to the **subverting** [changing] of the hearers.

NOTE THE CLEAR, STRONG STATEMENTS

1. CHARGING THEM BEFORE THE LORD - Command
2. STRIVE NOT ABOUT WORDS TO NO PROFIT - That is, to examine, read, and discuss the Bible, just to be doing it.
3. BUT TO THE SUBVERTING - Changing - converting or developing the hearers.
4. STUDY (THAT IS, GIVE DILIGENCE) - or really get into it - to master the principles, in order
5. TO BECOME A WORKMAN - a doer, a teacher - someone who is able to perform the act commanded.
6. BEFORE GOD - UNASHAMED, which means that we have confidence in what the Bible teaches and how to perform, obey and teach the principle by both being able to explain and practice it in our lives.

Principle Two

THE PROPER METHOD OF GROWING IN FAITH

One grows in faith by doing spiritual exercises daily.

"...*as* **a man thinketh in his heart, so is he:...**" (Proverbs 23:7).

This verse is one of the greatest BIOLOGICAL, PSYCHOLOGICAL, and BIBLICAL PRINCIPLES IN THE WORLD.

What a person thinks or what a person is on the inside is the type of person he really is, and will dictate the type of life he will manifest on the outside.

- If one TAKES INTO HIS MIND negative, worldly thoughts, then he WILL LIVE A NEGATIVE WORLDLY LIFE.

- If one TAKES INTO HIS MIND positive thoughts of faith, then HE WILL LIVE A POSITIVE LIFE OF FAITH.

- One CAN CHANGE A POOR SELF-IMAGE by developing good, positive thoughts.

- One CAN STRENGTHEN ONESELF AND INCREASE FAITH by doing three things:

1. Majoring on good, healthy thoughts.
2. Washing one's mind by reading and memorizing scriptures.
3. Stating right objectives and positive goals daily.

One can develop a good, happy inner self by this simple daily exercise. (Be sure to check the appropriated block each day.)

A MUST! **REPEAT THE DAILY DECLARATIONS FOUND AT THE END OF THE LESSONS AT LEAST EVERY MORNING AND EVENING.**

A MUST! **STRIVE TO MEMORIZE THE MEMORY VERSE EACH WEEK**

Principle Three

THE PROPER METHOD IN DEVELOPING A GOOD PRAYER LIFE

How to Begin Your Prayer:
OUR FATHER IN HEAVEN

With knowledge that the Bible commands each disciple to pray regularly and with a desire to pray more consistently in order to secure definite results, I now make the following prayer list.

Pray for these things.

1. **I'll pray for myself** - for a humble, submissive spirit towards Christ.
2. **For my family** - that I may be a Christian testimony and a blessing to each one of them.
3. **For my pastor** - that God will give him the grace, spiritual power and wisdom to lead, feed and shepherd the flock.
4. **For my country** - that God will send revival to our nation, especially to those in high positions.
5. **For our missionaries** - for their safety, success, and support. (Write down the missionaries' names and their countries.)

1. _____
Country: _____
2. _____

Country: _____
3. _____
Country: _____

6. **For my lost loved ones and friends** - Write down at least four people for whom you will pray daily.

   1. _____
      Date prayer answered: _____
   2. _____
      Date prayer answered: _____
   3. _____
      Date prayer answered: _____
   4. _____
      Date prayer answered: _____

7. **For evangelists and other special workers**, and call them by name.
Example: James Wilkins

How to conclude:
IN JESUS' NAME (authority), AMEN.

NOTE: Find a private place so you **will pray aloud**. In doing you will not be inhibited in praying for people or in public. Remember, prayer is a way of **ministering to others** as well as communing with God.

Principle Four

THE PROPER METHOD OF RETAINING BIBLE TRUTH

RETENTION
WILL IT BE 6% OR 62%

Do you want to learn? It is really up to you!!

These lessons were designed so you can maximize your ability to learn and remember what you have learned.

6%

If you read an article once, chances are you will not remember much about it after a period of time. In reading an article, the average person can only recall 6% of what he read just two weeks earlier.

If, however, you read the article and review it for six consecutive days, the average retention goes up to 62%.

62%

To maximize your retention, the following method of study is given. On the first day, read your lesson for Monday and fill in Monday's blanks. On Tuesday, reviews Monday's questions before reading Tuesday's lesson and filling in Tuesday's answers. Follow this pattern for the entire week.

Learn-and-Do material is designed to put the student into the Word everyday.

Principle Five

IT CREATES THE PROPER METHOD OF CONTROLLING THE FLESH.

When a person is born of the Spirit, he receives a **second nature,** A DIVINE NATURE. This nature is in addition to his human, fleshly nature.

When a person becomes a Christian, his human, fleshly nature IS NOT CHANGED AT ALL. The average believer knows little or nothing about the two-fold nature of the child of God.

The new convert is excited and thrilled over becoming a Christian, but after the newness and excitement wears off, many backslide or, at best, become a "normal" Christian. This method of Study-To-Learn-and-Do puts the student into the Word everyday where he feeds his inward man. Feeding the spiritual man, while starving the flesh, is **the only way to control the flesh.**

STUDY-TO-LEARN-AND-DO SERIES

HOW CAN WE CORRECT THE PROBLEM?

There is no way to correct the problem in the 45 minutes which is designated for teaching in Sunday school. With the prayer requests, introduction and recognition of visitors, the record keeping and announcements, much of that time is used. The rest of the class is given to lecturing (students listening) or discussion. The average person remembers very little of what he reads or hears one time. The sad result is little change or interest among the attendees.

THE METHOD OF INVOLVEMENT MUST CHANGE

- The material (the Bible) is the best
- Most of the teachers are excellent
- Most of the class members are sincere and want to grow Spiritually
- The needs of our lives are many

THE SOLUTION!

- Change to a proven method which enhances study and learning in people
- Motivate people to study the material at home
- Create more interest and class involvement during the class
- Produce real change and growth in the lives of the class members

- Develop students to the level of WORKMAN-Doers of the Word-Performers

STUDY-TO-LEARN-AND-DO-SERIES

A Sunday school and teaching method which succeeds in involving the individual members;
- To read the lesson
- To look up and write down "Key principles"
- To study the lesson material
- To retain a high percentage of the lesson in order to **OBEY** (the Word) and **DO**

This Learn-To-Do series is designated to follow the principles of how the brain learns. Medical science has learned that if the average person reads something one time that the average brain can only recall 6% of what it reads-two weeks later!! But if that same person reads the same information for 6 consecutive days, the average brain can recall 62% of the material.

The student is challenged to study the lesson for 10 minutes each week night in his home.

Monday: He reads the daily exercises and looks up the "Key principles" and writes them down in the answer blanks for that day.

Tuesday: He begins his study time by taking 2 minutes to review Monday's answers, and then he reads and completes the primary principles which he writes down in the answer blanks for Tuesday.

Wednesday: He begins his study time by taking 2

STUDY-TO-LEARN-AND-DO SERIES

minutes to review Monday's and Tuesday's answers, and then he takes 8-10 minutes to read and complete the answer blanks for Wednesday.

Thursday: He follows the same procedure.

Friday: He follows the same procedure. **NOTE**: If at all possible and for best results review the complete question blanks on Saturday.

GRADING PROCEDURE

If the student does the five daily exercises on the day assigned, he gives himself an "A".

If the student does all the answers but not on the day assigned, he gives himself a "B".

If the student does not complete all the exercises he gives himself the grade of "J" which reminds the student that he will take his final test at the judgment seat.

TO OBTAIN THE BEST RESULTS IN THE LIVES OF THE CLASS MEMBERS! SUNDAY MORNING OR CLASS PERIOD

Teachers: Do not attempt to teach the materials in the lesson during the class time. Reinforce and follow the method will embed "Key principles" in the mind and life of the participant. One does this by using the test question section of the lesson **ONLY,** during the class period.

1. Begin the class part of the time set aside for teaching by having the whole class turn to the test section.
2. Begin with question one for Monday.
3. Read the question until you come to the first blank. Pause, allowing all members of the class to give in unison the proper answer.
4. Continue on reading the question until you come to the next blank. Pause, allowing all of the class members to give the answer.
5. Do this for the complete five questions which make up Monday's test section. The five questions are "Key principles" which are the most important or foundational truths of that section. Take 3 or 4 minutes to discuss and enforce the "Key principles" then move on to the next day's activity.
6. Follow the same procedure for the ensuing four days exercises.
7. **Please take special note: The teacher teaches people, not lessons.** One part of the five sets of questions may be more pertinent for your people (class) than are the other four. If this is true in one of the lessons, then one should alter the procedure by skipping that day's activity when you come to it. Do the day's activity before and the day's activity following. After completing the other 4 day's activity (test questions)

come back and **spend the bulk of the class period on the day which was skipped.**
8. By following this procedure the teacher encourages the students to study each day's activity in order to make an "A", while giving the teacher the liberty to teach as the Holy Spirit may direct.

LESSON ONE

THE GREAT COMMISSION IN PROPORTION

"And Jesus came and spake unto them, saying, All power is given unto me in heaven and in earth. Go ye therefore, and teach all nations, baptizing them in the name of the Father, and of the Son, and of the Holy Ghost: Teaching them to observe all things whatsoever I have commanded you: and, lo, I am with you alway, even unto the end of the world. Amen."
(Matthew 28:18-20)

THE LESSON'S OUTLINE

I. **THE COMMISSION GIVEN TO THE CHURCH**
   A. The emphasis is on discipleship.
   B. The emphasis is on procedure.
   C. The emphasis is on getting the job done.

II. **THE PREACHERS GIVEN TO THE SAINTS**
   A. Who is responsible for developing the Saints?
   B. How are the Preachers to develop the Saints?

III. **THE APOSTLE PAUL GIVE AS AN EXAMPLE**
   A. Paul's testimony of why he was saved.
   B. Paul's example as a successful Christian.

C. Paul's example of developing Soul-winners.

IV. THE SAINTS GIVEN TO THE MINISTRY
  A. Started in "Teaching them to observe."
  B. II Timothy 2:2 reveals a Personal Revolving Commission.
  C. Peter's Command to the Believer, "Give an answer."
  D. You are to become a Teacher

THE LESSON'S PURPOSE

The stress in Matthew's account of the Great Commission is on "Making Disciple" and on teaching them to observe or Practice. The emphasis is on Method or Procedure (See summary).

THE LESSON'S MEMORY VERSES
Matthew 28:18-20

THE GREAT COMMISSION IN PROPORTION
(Matthew 28:18-20)
MONDAY

INTRODUCTION: There is only one Great Commission in the Bible! (+) But in order to understand the Great Commission one must study the Great Commission as presented by each of the writers of Matthew, Mark, Luke, John, and the Book of Acts. (+) Matthew was politically and legalistically orientated, so he presented Jesus as the "king." (+) Matthew's presentation of the Great

Lesson One 27

Commission begins with:
- (1) The Authority (power, exousia);
- (2) The Proper Procedure of doing the work (make disciples, baptize, and then develop them);
- (3) The Length of the Responsibility (unto the end of the age).

The emphasis in the Book of Matthew is on procedure or proper Methodology. (+) "Teach them to observe" or do "all things" I commanded you. (+) We will study this method of teaching them to observe, the method of developing the disciples under four headings.

I. THE COMMISSION GIVEN TO THE CHURCH
II. THE PREACHERS GIVEN TO THE SAINTS
III. THE APOSTLE PAUL GIVEN AS AN EXAMPLE
IV. THE SAINTS GIVEN TO THE WORK OF THE MINISTRY

TUESDAY

I. THE COMMISSION GIVE TO THE CHURCH
   A. **Our emphasis is on discipling**, not on theology.(+) Since this lesson is on discipling and not on theology, may we limit our comments to…Jesus setting up a local

unit during His personal ministry with its primary purpose of discipling.
B. **Our emphasis is on order or procedure**. In order to develop, train, direct, and motivate in this age-long task of preaching the Gospel to every creature there must be a central agency in charge of this training. (+)
C. **Our emphasis is on getting the job done**. In the Old Testament the Jewish nation was God's chosen people. They were to lead the work of evangelization of the world. God's method is this age is for a local church with a native pastor reaching his own nationality or kind. (+) People of the same race with the same background will respond to their own much better than to anyone else. With Jesus as its head, the Bible as its rule of faith, the Holy Spirit as its guide, and world evangelization as its goal, the local church can succeed in any area. (+)

WEDNESDAY

II. **THE PREACHERS GIVEN TO THE SAINTS**
   A. **Who is responsible for developing the members?** In Ephesians 4:11, the Bible declares that God gave preachers to the local church in order to develop the membership. (+)
      1. NOTE – Evangelist – Pastors – Teachers…(ministerial gifts).

Lesson One

    2. WHY? For the "perfecting of the saints." (verse 12) (+)
        a. Perfecting, equipping, developing, training, bringing to maturity.
        b. Who? "Saints" – you are either a saint or you ain't – SAVED or NOT SAVED.
    3. For the WORK of the MINISTRY:
        a. What is the work of the ministry? First, the saints are to win souls, then teach them to observe or do all things. (+)

B. How are the Preachers to develop the membership in soul-winning?
    1. They are to teach and develop by way of their example.
        a. Jesus began both TO DO and TO TEACH. (Acts 1:1) (+)
        b. In this important task, the pastors are to be examples, I Peter 5:3, "...being ensamples to the flock." They are over the flock, Acts 20:28.
        c. The membership is to submit to the pastor's example, leadership, and training, Heb. 13:7, (+) "...whose faith follow, considering the end of their conversation [life]." "Obey them that have rule over you, and submit yourselves;..." Heb. 13:17

THURSDAY

III. THE APOSTLE PAUL GIVEN AS AN EXAMPLE

A. **Paul's testimony of why he was saved.**
   1. "…for this cause I obtain mercy,…" I Tim. 1:16.
   2. "…in me…might shew forth…for a pattern…." This statement teaches that God saved Paul and made his life a pattern or example. (+)
   3. To whom? "…them which…hereafter believe…."

B. **Paul was one of the most successful Christians** who ever lived. (+) We should imitate his life as well as believe and quote his teachings. It is not enough to say, "Paul said." We must also imitate that which "Paul did."

C. **Paul's example of training (developing) soul-winners.**
   1. Paul's 20-20 vision – Acts 20:20.
      a. Kept back nothing which was profitable, but he went night and day with tears, Acts 20:31. Perfect example of dedication.
      b. Shewed and taught them publicly, then he would show and teach them from house to house (on-the-job training).
   2. Paul taught God's method of training others to win souls. (+)

      a. Jesus sent them out two-by-two, (+) Mark 6:7. One of the two was in charge of the visitation team: training the other member of the team in this important business of getting sinners saved from hell.
      b. First, it was Barnabas and Saul. Paul was in training – later it became Paul and Barnabas. Paul and Silas, and then Paul and literally thousands of others whom Paul trained (on-the-job training from house to house) as well as showing them publically (soul-winning demonstration). Paul taught them so well that they too became soul-winning trainers and taught others. (+)

FRIDAY

IV. THE SAINTS GIVEN TO THE WORK OF THE MINISTRY

The local church (made up of people) was commissioned to make disciples or win souls, (+) but their responsibility did not end there. They were to teach the ones they won, to "observe" or "do all things" that Jesus commanded. (+) Therefore, the members are to be teachers, trainers, and developers.

A. **Stated in Matthew 28:20,** Jesus commanded them to teach others all things that they had been taught of Him.
B. **II Tim. 2:2 reveals a personal revolving commission,** which has finally reached YOU! (+) "And the things that thou [Timothy] hast heard of me [Apostle Paul] among many witnesses [believers], the same commit thou to faithful men, who shall be able to teach others, also."
   1. There are four responsible teachers in this verse:
      a. Paul taught Timothy.
      b. Timothy taught faithful men.
      c. Faithful men taught others.
      d. Others are to teach others…
   2. What were the others to do? It is inferred that they should begin the circle of teaching all over again. The revolving circle of one generation teaching another generation has finally reached YOU!
C. **Peter commands the believer to** SANCTIFY the PRINCIPLE OF SOUL-WINNING (I Peter 3:15). (+)
   1. SANCTIFY means "set apart," master, get hold of.
   2. THE LORD GOD IN YOUR HEARTS means to master the plan of Salvation, the principles of Salvation so you may…
      a. GIVE AN ANSWER.
      b. To whom – EVERY MAN.
      c. Of what? THE HOPE YOU HAVE.

Lesson One

        d. How? WITH MEEKNESS AND FEAR.
    3. You cannot escape your responsibility simply because you are fearful or scared.
  D. **You are to become a teacher**.
    1. Hebrews 5:12, for the time when you ought to be TEACHERS.
    2. You incur the displeasure of God by drawing back. Heb. 10:39, the choice is either, believe to the saving of your life, or drawback to perdition or destruction.

SUMMARY: The Bible teaches method as strongly as it teaches doctrine. (+) Why limit the beautiful doctrine of God's Word to missions, the method of mass evangelism? Pastors and evangelists were given to the saints in order to develop them (by example) in the ministry of winning souls and training those who are won to win souls. This is done through public teaching and showing, followed by on-the-job training by the soul-winner-trainer and silent partner-trainee teams. If we will get back to the New Testament methods, we will have New Testament (Book of Acts) results.

Procedure of obtaining and retaining the most from this lesson:

Monday -Read the entire lesson through and then fill-in the blanks for Monday. Do prayer time and daily declaration.

Tuesday - Re-read the material for Tuesday and fill in the blanks. Review the questions and blanks for Monday. Do prayer time and daily declaration.

Wednesday - Do same – review blanks for Monday and Tuesday. Do prayer time and daily declaration.

Thursday - Do same – review for Monday, Tuesday, and Wednesday. Do prayer time and daily declaration.

Friday - Do same – review for Monday, Tuesday, Wednesday, and Thursday. Do prayer time and daily declaration.

*Read an article one time and retain 6% in two weeks – read for six consecutive days and retain 62%.

Lesson One   35

MONDAY – INTRODUCTION

1. There is only _____ Great _____ in the Bible!

2. One must study the _____ Commission as presented by _____ of the writers of _____, _____, _____, John, and the Book of _____.

3. Matthew was politically and legalistically orientated, so he presented _____ as the _____.

4. The _____ in the Book of Matthew is on _____ or proper _____.

5. "Teach them to _____" or _____ "all things" I have commanded you.

TUESDAY –
THE COMMISSION GIVEN

1. Our emphasis is on _____, not on theology.

2. There must be a _____ agency in charge of this _____.

3. God's method in this age is for a _____ _____ with a native preacher reaching his own nationality or kind.

4. With Jesus as its _____, the _____ as its rule of faith, the _____ _____ as its guide, and world _____ as its goal, the local _____ can succeed in any area.

Lesson One

WEDNESDAY –
THE PREACHERS GIVEN TO THE SAINTS

1. The Bible declares that God gave _____ to the local _____ in order to develop the _____.

2. Why did God give evangelists, pastors, and teachers to the local church? For the "_____ _____ _____ _____."

3. First the _____ are to win souls, then teach them to _____ or _____ all things.

4. Jesus began both to _____ and to _____.

5. The membership is to submit to the pastor's _____, _____, and _____.

THURSDAY –
THE APOSTLE PAUL GIVEN AS AN EXAMPLE

1. God saved Paul and made his _____ a pattern or _____.

2. _____ was one of the most _____ Christians who ever lived.

3. Paul taught _____ method of training others to win _____.

4. Jesus sent them out _____ _____ _____.

5. Paul taught them so well that they too became _____ _____ _____ and _____ others.

Lesson One   39

FRIDAY –
THE SAINTS GIVEN TO
THE WORK OF THE MINISTRY

1. The local church (made up of people) was commissioned to _____ _____ or_____ _____.

2. They were to _____ the ones they won, to "_____" or _____ all things" that Jesus commanded.

3. II Timothy 2:2 reveals a _____ revolving commission, which has finally reached _____!

4. Peter commands the believer to _____ the PRINCIPLE OF _____ _____.

5. The Bible teaches _____ as strongly as it teaches _____.

DAILY DECLARATION

I will strive to become more active in the worldwide commission to my church.

MEMORY VERSE

"And the things that thou hast heard of me among many witnesses, the same commit thou to faithful men, who shall be able to teach others also." II Timothy 2:2

Check Box after Repeating

Monday	Tuesday	Wednesday	Thursday	Friday

MY COMMITMENT

I will strive to do the things which the Great Commission teaches that I, as a member, should do.

Name_____

Date _____

LESSON TWO

THE GREAT COMMISSION AND ITS PERSONNEL

"And he said unto them, Go ye into all the world, and preach the gospel to every creature." (Mark 16:15)

THE LESSON'S OUTLINE

I. INDIVIDUAL WITNESSING BY EVERY BELIEVER IS THE ORDAINED WAY
  A. Jesus said, "I have chosen and ordained you."
  B. Jesus ordained them to win souls.

II. INDIVIDUAL WITNESSING BY EVERY BELIEVER IS THE ASSURED WAY
  A. God's promise (assurance) to the Believer.
  B. God's promise leads to the abundant life.

III. INDIVIDUAL WITNESSING BY THE BELIEVER IS THE HISTORICAL WAY
  A. The going believers (from house to house).
  B. The scattered believers (everywhere preaching).
  C. The Twelve believers (reached Asia in twenty-four months).

IV. INDIVIDUAL WITNESSING IS THE PERPETUAL WAY

A. Most can go!
B. Some can stay.
C. All are witnesses.

THE LESSON'S PURPOSE
The stress in Mark's account of the Great Commission is that every single believer IS TO BE A WITNESS.

THE LESSON'S MEMORY VERSE
Mark 16:15

THE GREAT COMMISSION AND ITS PURPOSE
(Mark 16:15)

MONDAY

INTRODUCTION: The Holy Spirit chose Mark, the writer of the Gospel of Mark, to present Jesus as a servant. (+) A servant is not interested in genealogies, legalities, or proper order in an age long commission. He is interested in WHAT HE, PERSONALLY, IS SUPPOSE TO DO. Whom am I suppose to serve? What is my job? (+) So Mark's interpretation of the Great Commission is, GO INTO ALL THE WORLD AND PREACH THE GOSPEL TO EVERY CREATURE. (+) God would not command something that WAS IMPOSSIBLE.

Lesson Two 43

This direct command from the lips of Jesus can only be OBEYED when two things happen.

First, when the redeemed or saved realize that Jesus meant what He said. This generation is charged or commissioned to preach the Gospel to every creature who is alive today. (+)

Second, the only possible way this command can be obeyed is that every single believer is to "take this command seriously" (+) and "preach the Gospel to every creature" in his own personal world. This lesson has to do with the PERSONNEL of the Great Commission.

TUESDAY

I. **INDIVIDUAL WITNESSING BY EVERY BELIEVER IS THE ORDAINED WAY**
   A. Jesus said, I have chosen and ORDAINED you. (+) (John 15:16)
      1. Most people do not understand what Jesus means in this verse because they do not consider to whom He is speaking.
      2. Jesus is speaking to the disciples, not to the Holy Spirit. (+)
   B. What were they ordained to do?
      1. TO "GO!" There are 168 hours in every week. The child of God was chosen and ordained to use some of that time going

to the lost with the message of Salvation every week. (+)
2. BRING FORTH FRUIT – The fruit referred to here is not the fruit of the Holy Spirit mentioned in Galatians 5:22, but it is the fruit of the saved or righteous as stated in Proverbs 11:20 (+)
3. WHAT IS THE FRUIT OF THE SAVED? "The fruit of the righteous **is** a tree of life; and he that winneth **souls is wise**. (+)

WEDNESDAY

II. INDIVIDUAL WITNESSING BY EVERY BELIEVER IS THE ASSURED WAY (+)
A. GOD'S PROMISE TO THE BELIEVER
  1. "He that goeth forth and weepeth, bearing precious seed, shall doubtless come again with rejoicing, bringing his sheaves [souls] with him." (Psalms 126:6)
     a. NOTICE – "SHALL" is a definite promise to the one who goes (+) (burdened with the Word) – DOUBTLESS come again with rejoicing (absolute promise from Almighty God).
     b. NOTICE – "HE" is not a preacher. (+) It is not someone who has a gift of gab. It is not someone who has a special calling. (+) It is just HE (anyone)...

Lesson Two

      c. NOTICE – "WITH REJOICING" – there are four descriptive terms of the joy the soul-winner will have. (+)
         1. "...like them that dream." (Psalms 126:1).
         2. "...mouth filled with laughter,..." (Psalms 126:2)
         3. "...tongue with singing:..." (Psalms 126:2)
         4. Heathen said, "...The LORD hath done great things for them. The LORD has done great things for us; whereof we are glad." (Psalms 126:2-3)

  2. THIS VERSE PROMISES THE ABUNDANT LIFE
      a. It states that anyone who goes with a concern for souls – with a message from the Word.
      b. Will doubtless come again. With abundant victorious life, like them that dreamed, mouth filled with laughter, tongue with singing, everyone noticed the blessings of God upon their life. They acknowledge God's blessings "whereof we are glad."

  3. FIVE SIMPLE STEPS

You are not only ordained to go and bring forth fruit, but God gave the simple steps to bearing fruit, which brings the abundant life. (+) The steps are:

a. GOING – to the lost.
b. WEEPING – concerned.
c. SOWING – the message.
d. HAVING FAITH – (doubtless) a sure promise.
e. REJOICING – because of souls won.

THURSDAY

III. INDIVIDUAL WITNESSING BY EVERY BELIEVER IS THE HISTORICAL WAY

The method the disciples used to evangelize cities in the Book of Acts is very evident. (+)

A. The BELIEVERS went from house to house. (+) "…they [believers] ceased not to teach and preach Jesus Christ" (soul-winning). Where? IN EVERY HOUSE! (Acts 2:46-47, 5:42, 20:20)
B. The SCATTERED BELIEVERS went everywhere preaching the Word in Acts 8:1-4. Acts 8:1 tells how everyone, except the twelve apostles, were run out of the city of Jerusalem. In Acts 8:4, it tells that they (BELIEVERS) went everywhere preaching (SOUL-WINNING). (+)
C. The TWELVE BELIEVERS, when trained, reached Asia in twenty-four months. (+) (Acts 19:1-10). In verse seven, Paul said, "And all the men [disciples] were about twelve." Then the startling success of their

witnessing is announced in verse ten. Under the leadership of Paul, and the nine preachers with him (Paul, Silas, Dr. Luke and the seven preachers mentioned in Acts 20:4) were able to train the twelve members whose number multiplied until everyone in an area as large as the state of New Mexico, were evangelized. **(+) (All Asia) in two years.** Acts 19:10

FRIDAY

IV. INDIVIDUAL WITNESSING IS THE PERPETUAL WAY

The Commission given by Jesus to His church was an age long commission, which is still in force today. (+) How can a local church expect all of its members to be obedient to this personal command to individuals? In order to be obedient and feel like a part of the local church team, one must understand the place where they fit in and what they can personally do to be an effective witness for their Savior.

The experience that David and his men had is recorded in the book of I Samuel, Chapter 30, which illustrates the proper working of a church. David and his men were sent to rescue their families and friends who had been taken captive by the enemy. The total army of six hundred worked together as a team. **(+)** Four hundred pursued after and were active in the going while two hundred stayed by the stuff. The four hundred went forth into active combat in order to rescue those who were in captivity. The two hundred were not physically able to go. They stayed by the stuff. In the story it indicates that the ones who stayed by the stuff were scared, thinking that their loved ones would die or have something worse than death happen to them so they fasted and prayed while the four hundred went out to rescue the helpless captives.

This teaches that MOST CAN GO while some are to stay by the stuff. This shows that ALL are important and ARE NEEDED in the team effort to rescue the lost.

THEY SHALL PART ALIKE

Some of the four hundred who went to battle and won the release of the captives did not believe that the two hundred who stayed by the stuff should receive any of the spoils or rewards.

King David forcefully established an ordinance which became permanent (I Samuel 30:23-24).

> "Then said David, Ye shall not do so, my brethren, with that which the LORD hath given us, who hath preserved us,

Lesson Two 49

and delivered the company that came against us into our hand. For who will hearken unto you in this matter? but as his part is that goeth down to the battle, so shall his part be that tarrieth by the stuff: they shall part alike."

Notice the wording of the ordinances, "but as his part is that goeth down to the battle (spiritual battle or winning souls), so shall his part be that tarrieth by the stuff, THEY SHALL PART ALIKE.

    A. MOST CAN GO! Many people could get involved in the church's outreach program. They can set aside at least two hours each week and go out and witness to people. (+) In order to overcome the fear and uncertainty, which this causes in the average person's mind, many would begin as a silent partner in the visitation team. If a person would go a few times they would soon experience the joy and happiness that their obedience to Christ's command causes. A person would soon look forward to that "special time" each week. They would soon become "soul conscious" and accept their personal responsibility to witness. Everyone could telephone someone, cards of invitation could be sent, and the neighbors next door could be invited. The fellow employee needs

someone to encourage and invite him. A little child would respond to love and encouragement.
- B. SOME CAN STAY! Some of David's men were not physically able to go. (+) Their King told them to stay by the stuff. No doubt many prayers and tears were offered up to God on behalf of the comrades who were able to go and rescue their families and friends. They were just as dedicated to their responsibility of staying by "the stuff" as were the ones who were able to go. This truth is taught by the fact that both those that went forth and those that stayed by "the stuff" were rewarded equally. This story just illustrates that everyone has a job and a part. The church desperately needs members to stay by the stuff. Through turning the TV off and spending each Thursday night in praying for those who are able to go. Many could be active in praying for the visitation teams daily.
- C. ALL ARE WITNESSES! Every believer is a witness. Some are a good testimony of what a Christian is. Some believer's lifestyle and behavior is a bad testimony for Christ. You are either someone's example or encouragement to come to Christ or you are someone's excuse for not coming to Christ. (+) Each one of us are either obedient to the Great Commission or we are disobedient.

Lesson Two

SUMMARY: The Bible teaches METHOD as strongly as it teaches DOCTRINE. God's method of evangelizing a community is that every member (believer) of a local church is to be trained and developed so they can evangelize every creature in their own little personal world. We train these people by showing and teaching them publicly and by taking them out and showing them from house to house (on-the-job training). They are to be trained until they are able to train others.

Procedure of obtaining and retaining the most from this lesson:

Monday - Read the entire lesson through and then fill-in the blanks for Monday. Do prayer time and daily declaration.

Tuesday - Re-read the material for Tuesday and fill in the blanks. Review the questions and blanks for Monday. Do prayer time and daily declaration.

Wednesday - Do same – review blanks for Monday and Tuesday. Do prayer time and daily declaration.

Thursday - Do same – review for Monday, Tuesday, and Wednesday. Do prayer time and daily declaration.

Friday - Do same – review for Monday, Tuesday, Wednesday, and Thursday. Do prayer time and daily declaration.

MONDAY – INTRODUCTION

1. The Holy Spirit chose _____, the writer of the Gospel of Mark, to present _____ as a

   servant.

2. A servant asks himself, "Whom am _____ suppose to _____? _____ is my job?"

3. "_____ into _____ the world and preach the _____ to _____

   creature.

4. This generation is charged or commissioned to preach the _____ to every creature who is _____ today.

5. Every _____ believer is to take this command _____.

Lesson Two

TUESDAY – THE ORDAINED WAY

1. Jesus said, "I have chosen and _____ you."

2. Jesus is speaking to the _____ , not to the Holy _____ .

3. The child of God was _____ and _____ to use some of that

   _____ going to the lost with the message of Salvation every week..

4. Bring forth _____ is defined in Proverbs 11: _____ .

5. "He that _____ souls is wise," is _____ answer.

WEDNESDAY – THE ASSURED WAY

1. Individual _____ by every believer is the _____ way.

2. Notice – "_____" - is a definite promise to the one who goes.

3. Notice – "HE" is not _____. It is not someone who has a special _____.

4. There are four _____ terms of the _____ the soul-winner will have.

5. God _____ the simple _____ to bearing fruit, which brings the abundant _____.

Lesson Two   55

THURSDAY – THE HISTORICAL WAY

1. The _____ the disciples used to _____ cities in the book of Acts is very evident.

2. The _____ went from house to house.

3. In Acts 8:4, it tells that they (_____) went everywhere preaching (SOUL-WINNING).

4. The _____ believers, when trained, reached _____ in twenty-four months.

5. This area was as large as the state of New _____.

FRIDAY – THE PERPETUAL WAY

1. The Commission given by Jesus to His church was an _____ long commission, which

    is still in force _____.

2. The total _____ of six hundred worked together as a _____.

3. They could set aside at _____ two _____ each _____ and go

    out and witness to people.

4. Some of David's men were not _____ able to go.

5. You are either someone's _____ or encouragement to come to Christ or you are someone's _____ for not coming to Christ.

Lesson Two

DAILY DECLARATION

I will strive to submit to God's purpose for my life and become fruitful.

MEMORY VERSE

"The fruit of the righteous is a tree of life; and he that winneth souls is wise." Proverbs 11:30

Check Box after Repeating

Monday	Tuesday	Wednesday	Thursday	Friday

MY COMMITMENT

I will commit to become part of my church's visitation program.

Name_____

Date _____

LESSON THREE

THE GREAT COMMISSION IN PERSPECTIVE

"And said unto them, Thus it is written, and thus it behoved Christ to suffer, and to rise from the dead the third day: And that repentance and remission of sins should be preached in his name among all nations, beginning at Jerusalem. And ye are witnesses of these things. And, behold, I send the promise of my Father upon you: but tarry ye in the city of Jerusalem, until ye be endued with power from on high."
Luke 24:46-49

THE LESSON'S OUTLINE
1. **The Gospel is to be proclaimed**
   a. What is primary?
   b. What is needed?
   c. What is the Gospel?
      i. Defined in I Corinthians 15:1-4
      ii. The power of God unto salvation
      iii. The disciples are to proclaim the Gospel

2. **The Gospel is Jesus Christ and Him crucified**
   a. The message is positive
   b. The message is not negative

3. **The Gospel is for all men**
   a. To be preached in all nations

b. To be preached-emphasis on the message of the Gospel

THE LESSON'S PURPOSE

The stress in Luke's account of the great commission is on the message which is to be proclaimed in all the world. (See summary)

THE LESSON'S MEMORY VERSES

"For I am not ashamed of the gospel of Christ: for it is the power of God unto salvation to every one that believeth; to the Jew first, and also to the Greek."
Romans 1:16

THE GREAT COMMISSION IN PERSPECTIVE

Luke 24:46-49

Lesson Three

MONDAY

INTRODUCTION

The beloved physician, Dr. Luke, a companion of Apostle Paul, and may have been the only Gentile that the Holy Spirit used in writing the Bible, presents the great commission in perspective. +He agrees with Matthew and Mark concerning the commission's scope; the message of salvation is to be preached in all nations beginning with Jerusalem. +Dr. Luke is not so concerned with the authority to preach or in what order the church program is to be administered, he is interested in the message and power which will make genuine disciples. +He stresses the message and the endowment or enabling power of the Holy Spirit. He represents Jesus as the Son of Man; therefore, as a good family physician, he is more interested in saving his patient's life than in having the legal authority to perform surgery. +By perspective, we mean a deeper look into, or a prescription which will bring the desired results. When one is obedient and does as the Bible commands, what message should he give and which power should he depend upon, in order to realize the Divine results of making disciples.

TUESDAY

THE GOSPEL IS TO BE PROCLAIMED

A. WHAT IS PRIMARY?

What is primary or first work of the church? Many seem to believe that the church's job is to defend the faith or the Bible. This position causes the attitude and mind set to be defensive. The primary stress in the commission is positive, not negative. This defensive attitude may degenerate into argumentative and become critical. +

The primary stress in the commission is positive, not negative. + Please note the proper stress.

1. Matthew 28:19: to teach all nations by getting them saved, and then baptizing them.
2. Mark 16:15: to preach the Gospel, and then baptize new converts.
3. Luke 24:47: to preach repentance and remission of sin.

B. WHAT IS NEEDED?
The sinner does not need to be straightened out, he needs to be saved. He does not need to be argued with, he needs the Gospel. +
C. WHAT IS THE GOSPEL?

1. In I Corinthians 15:1-4 Paul defines the Gospel. It is, Christ died for our sins according to the Scriptures and that He was buried and rose again the third day according to the Scriptures.
2. The Gospel is the power of God unto salvation to everyone who believeth. Romans 1:16 +

Lesson Three

3. What Jesus commanded the disciples to proclaim to the world is...Jesus died and was raised again so the sinner could repent and have remission of his sins through His name. +

WEDNESDAY

THE GOSPEL IS JESUS CHRIST AND HIM CRUCIFIED

A. THE MESSAGE IS POSITIVE

1. THE MESSAGE FITS THE SETTING. "For I determined not to know any thing among you, save Jesus Christ, and him crucified." + I Corinthians 2:2 In order to understand THIS STATEMENT and properly interpret what the writer is saying, one MUST analyze;
   1) Who is speaking?
   2) To whom is he speaking?
   3) What is the time period he is referring to?
   4) What is the setting or the occasion?

     a. Who is speaking? The Apostle Paul.
     b. To whom is he speaking? The believers who constitute the Corinthian church. I Corinthians 1:1-2
     c. What time period was he referring to? He was referring to the time he came giving his testimony to the people when THEY WERE LOST. I Corinthians 2:1

    d. What was the setting or the occasion? PAUL CAME TO A LOST CITY AS A MISSIONARY to win people to Christ. + It was under this setting, presenting the simple plan of salvation that he said, For I determined not to know anything except Jesus Christ and Him crucified. A positive presentation of the plan of salvation to the lost which did its job of converting. He told young Timothy, "Preach the Word:..." (II Timothy 4:2) It is the clear setting forth of the plan of salvation which brings conviction and salvation to the lost. He set his mind to stay on the positive message of salvation. +

2. THE MESSAGE IS NOT NEGATIVE. Soul-winning is not making rebuttals to every false ideal and doctrine. Making rebuttals or answering arguments is not the Bible way to win souls.

    a.. Jesus stated that unless a man is born again he cannot see or perceive (understand) Spiritual things. John 3:3

    b. Paul said that the natural man (lost man) receiveth not the things of the Spirit. If the lost person cannot receive them, then why argue with him?

    c. They are foolishness unto him. If Spiritual things are foolishness unto the sinner, then why argue with him about the Spiritual things.

Lesson Three

> d. Neither can we know them. The unsaved cannot understand Spiritual things; there is no way he can know them because he has no Spiritual discernment. I Corinthians 2:14
> e. The only thing rebuttals and arguing will do for the sinner is hurt him. + DO NOT BE negative in the presentation of the plan of salvation. BE POSITIVE.

3. THE MESSAGE IS SIMPLE. It is Jesus Christ and Him crucified for the remission of sins. + If a man repents or turns from his sins and receives Jesus Christ as his Saviour he is saved.

THURSDAY

THE GOSPEL IS FOR ALL MEN

A. TO BE PREACHED IN ALL NATIONS Luke 24:47

> 1. God love the whole world so much that He sent his Son to die for all. (John 3:16)
> 2. Anyone who wants to can receive this gift of salvation (Romans 10:13) That means me and YOU, that means EVERYBODY!

B. THE EMPHASIS IN LUKE IS "THE GOSPEL".

1. **THERE IS ONLY ONE PLAN OF SALVATION** (Gospel). + There is not a plan of salvation for the lost Catholic, another for the lost Jew,+ and still another for the educated and still another, etc. There is only one simple Gospel story for all men to hear. If they believe it, they are saved. If they do not believe, they are lost.

2. **FOUR BASIC PRINCIPLES TO MAKE CLEAR** +

    a. The fact of sin. "…**all** have sinned…" Romans 3:23
    b. The consequence for sin. "…the wages of sin is death;…" Romans 6:23
    c. The remedy for sin. "But God commendeth…" Romans 5:8 Only one Jesus who died for sin.
    d. The individual response. "For whosoever…" Romans 10:13 It is not enough for a man to know that he is a sinner, who is going to hell, that Jesus died in his place so he may repent and be saved. HE MUST RESPOND! +

FRIDAY

MASTER THESE SIMPLE SCRIPTURES AND PRINCIPLES

a. The believer DOES NOT NEED ANY OTHER SCRIPTURE to be able to witness to EVERY MAN on the face of the earth.
b. Master the method of clearly presenting these four principles. + Learn how to illustrate these four spiritual principles so the Holy Spirit can illuminate the sinners mind. In doing so you will gain tremendous confidence and skill.
c. Submit to the Bible method of being a silent partner trainee and learn by going with a soul-winner who is winning souls. +

SUMMARY

The Bible teaches method just as clearly as it does doctrine. + The method of making disciples is to clearly present the Gospel to the lost. The Gospel first shows the need, the remedy and then demands a response. + We can teach people to clearly present the Gospel by teaching the four principles which are based in four simple Scriptures. Anyone can become a soul-winner if he uses God's method of training people to become soul-winners and restricts himself to teaching them to present Jesus Christ and Him crucified. +

Procedure of obtaining and retaining the

most from this lesson.

MONDAY-Read all of the lessons through and then fill in the blanks for Monday.
TUESDAY-Re-read the material for Tuesday and fill in the blanks. Review the questions and blanks for Monday.
WEDNESDAY-Do same-review blanks for Monday and Tuesday
THURSDAY-Do same-review blanks for Monday, Tuesday and Wednesday
FRIDAY-do same-review blanks for Monday, Tuesday, Wednesday and Thursday

*Read an article one time and retain 6% in two weeks-read for six consecutive days and retain 62%

Lesson Three   69

DAILY DECLARATION

I will strive to become a soul-winner by
memorizing how to present the four
Spiritual principles as I serve as a silent partner.

MEMORY VERSE

For I am not ashamed of the gospel of Christ: for it
is the power of God unto salvation to every one that
believeth; to the Jew first, and also to the Greek.
Romans 1:16

CHECK BLOCK AFTER REPEATING

Monday	Tuesday	Wednesday	Thursday	Friday

MY COMMITMENT

I will obey the great commission by dedicating time
in every week to participate in
my church's visitation program.

Name_____
Grade_____

MONDAY
INTRODUCTION

1. The beloved physician Dr. _____, may have been the only _____ to be used to write part of the bible.

2. The message of _____ was to be preached to all _____ beginning with _____.

3. He is interested in the _____ and _____ which will make real _____.

4. As a good family _____ he is interested in _____ his patients _____ than in having the _____ authority to perform surgery.

5. By _____, we mean a deeper _____ into or a prescription which will bring the desired _____.

Lesson Three   71
TUESDAY
THE GOSPEL IS TO BE PROCLAIMED

1. This defensive _____ may degenerate into _____ and become _____.

2. The _____ stress in the commission is _____, not negative.

3. He does not need to be _____ with; he needs the _____.

4. The Gospel is the _____ of God unto salvation to _____ who _____.

5. Jesus _____ so the _____ could repent and have _____ of sins through His _____.

WEDNESDAY
THE GOSPEL IS JESUS CHRIST AND HIM CRUCIFIED

1. I _____ not to know _____ among you save Jesus Christ, and Him _____.

2. Paul came to a _____ city as a _____ to win people.

3. He set his _____ to stay on the positive _____ of _____.

4. The _____ thing _____ and arguing with the sinner does is to _____ him.

5. It is _____ _____ and Him crucified for the remission of _____.

Lesson Three   73

THURSDAY
THE GOSPEL IS FOR ALL MEN

1. The Gospel is for all _____.

2. There is only _____ plan of salvation (Gospel)

3. There is not a plan of salvation for the lost _____ and another for the lost _____.

4. There are "Four basic" principles to _____ clear.

5. It is _____ enough for man to know he is a _____. He must _____!

FRIDAY
MASTER THESE SIMPLE…SUMMARY

1. Master the method of clearly presenting these _____ principles.

2. Submit to the _____ method of being a silent _____ trainee and learn by _____.

3. The Bible teaches _____ just as clearly as it does _____.

4. The _____ first shows the _____, the _____ and then demands a _____.

5. Anyone can become a _____.

LESSON FOUR

THE GREAT COMMISSION IN PARTICULAR

"Then said Jesus to them again, Peace be unto you: as my Father hath sent me, even so send I you. And when he had said this, he breathed on them, and saith unto them, Receive ye the Holy Ghost: Whose soever sins ye remit, they are remitted unto them; and whose soever sins ye retain, they are retained."
John 20:21-23

THE LESSON'S OUTLINE

I. **A VIVID PRESENTATION OF THE COMMISSION**
   A. Summed up in a Question – What would Jesus do?
   B. AS MY FATHER SENT ME.
   C. EVEN SO SEND I YOU.

II. **A VIVID POSTSCRIPT TO THE COMMISSION**
   A. The average reaction to the Commission.
   B. The postscript to John's Commission.
   C. How do men have power to remit sin?

III. **A VIVID INTERPRETATION OF THE COMMISSION**
   A. Paul was pure from the blood of all men.
   B. Israel had the blood of the innocent in her skirts.

    C. David pleaded, "Deliver me from blood-guiltiness."
    D. Their lives prove they felt their responsibility.

THE LESSON'S PURPOSE

The stress in John's account of the Great Commission is on the personal responsibility of the individual believer (+) to the lost and his power to either remit or retain SIN.

THE LESSON'S MEMORY VERSE
John 20:21-23

THE GREAT COMMISSION IN PARTICULAR
(John 20:21-23)

MONDAY

INTRODUCTION: **The average Christian does not feel** any sense of responsibility in carry out the Great Commission. Many members give some type of mission offering because of the Great Commission, but there seems to be very few believers who comprehend the magnitude of **their personal responsibility to the lost world. (+)**

Matthew presented the PROCEDURE for the Church to follow in making and developing disciples for world evangelization. Mark tells us the METHOD that must be followed. The individual

Lesson Four

believer is to witness to those in his individual world. Luke stresses the MESSAGE that must be presented in order to make genuine believers. John presents JESUS as the Son of God. As the Son of God, Jesus **felt the tremendous need of the lost.** (+) Their hopeless plight and the consuming consequences if they die lost. When John presented his view of the Great Commission given by Jesus, he passed this individual responsibility on to the believer. (+)

Years ago when D. L. Moody was first saved, he was presented to a Church board as a candidate for church membership. He was asked the question, "What has Jesus done for you in particular?" Young Dwight, who was nervous and untaught in the Scriptures, replied, "I know He has done a lot for us in general, but I cannot think of anything He has done for me in PARTICULAR."

Apostle John's account of the Great Commission attempts to take **the responsibility of the believer out of the general category** (+) and make the individual believer feel his responsibility to a lost world in PARTICULAR. (+)

TUESDAY

I. **A VIVID PRESENTATION OF THE COMMISSION**
   A. SUMMED UP IN THE QUESTION, "WHAT WOULD JESUS DO?" John shows his insight into his job as a Christian by

saying, "My job on earth is the same job God the Father gave His Son to do while He was on the earth."
- B. AS MY FATHER SENT ME.
    1. Why did God the Father send Jesus into the world? Jesus answers this question in Luke 19:10, "For the Son of man is come **to seek and to save** that which was lost." (+)
    2. The daily life of Jesus demonstrates why He came into the world.
        a. He won Nicodemus, the woman at the well, Zacharias, the thief on the Cross, and hundreds of others daily.
        b. He was teaching, developing, and encouraging others daily.
    3. Jesus sacrificed His life. The whole life of Jesus was lived for the benefit of others. He finally gave His life of the Cross for others.
    1. EVEN SO SEND I YOU. This is very clearly stated. "I, Jesus, am sending you to do the same things and for the same reason that my Father sent me."
    2. EVEN SO comes from the Greek, "Houtos Kai," which means in the same manner or in the manner previously described or illustrated.
    3. The Great Commission, according to John, simply **bypasses laws, procedures, technicalities, and speaks directly to the believer's heart.** (+) Whatever Jesus did in a given situation,

Lesson Four 79

is the same thing you should do. Jesus was totally committed to the SAVING of lost souls and to the development of believers.
   4. We need to die to self and present our body as a living sacrifice. (Romans 12:1) (+)

WEDNESDAY

II. **A VIVID POSTSCRIPT TO THE COMMISSION**
   A. THE AVERAGE REACTION TO THE COMMISSION
      1. Well, Jesus was divine, I am human. He was perfect and I am so imperfect. I know that verse said that, but you really can't expect me to GIVE UP everything and become a religious fanatic, can you?
      2. I will give some to missions. I believe if I do, that God will understand. (+) I will go to the Church myself. That's about all I can answer for...myself.
      3. If I get a chance, I will witness to some of my friends or even to some of the people I meet. I will pass out some tracts. I do pray for missionaries...when I remember. (+)
   B. THE POSTSCRIPT TO JOHN'S COMMISSION
      1. **From the lips of Jesus.** It seems as if Jesus anticipated all or our human

reasoning and excuses because He added a postscript to the Great Commission.
  2. **Stated in verse twenty-three...** "Whose soever sins you remit, they are remitted unto them; and whose soever sins ye retain, they are retained."
C. HOW DOES MAN HAVE POWER TO REMIT SINS?
  1. The postscript to the Great Commission teaches that man has power to remit sins. (+) But the question arises, "How does man have power to remit sins?"
  2. As the believer goes and presents the Plan of Salvation, prays for the sinner, and persuades him to call upon the name of Jesus, then his sins are remitted.
  3. If the believer fails to go – if he fails to pray – if the believer fails to persuade the sinner to call upon the Savior's name, then the sinner's sins are retained (+) and HE GOES TO HELL.
  4. This postscript shows the believer what his responsibility toward the lost really is. (+) It also shows him that **both God and the sinner need the believer** to turn away from his normal religious life to dedicate himself and **imitate the life of Jesus.**

THURSDAY

III. A VIVID INTERPRETATION OF THE COMMISSION

  A. PAUL WAS PURE FROM THE BLOOD OF ALL MEN (+) "Wherefore I take you to record this day, that I am pure from the blood of all [men]. For I have not shunned to declare unto you all the counsel of God." (Acts 20:26-27)

    1. What does it mean, "Pure from the blood of all men?" This phrase is defined in Ezekiel 3:18. God told Ezekiel that if he didn't warn the sinners and they died in their sins, then Ezekiel would **have their blood on his hands.** If he tried to win them and they would not listen, then they were responsible for their own condition and Ezekiel WAS PURE FROM THEIR BLOOD.

    2. Paul said he was pure from their blood because he had declared unto to them the whole counsel of God. He had warned them night and day with tears for the space of three years. (Acts 20:3)

  B. ISRAEL HAD THE BLOOD OF THE SOULS OF THE POOR INNOCENTS IN THEIR SKIRTS. "Also in thy skirts is found the blood of the souls of the poor innocents: I have not found it by secret search, but upon all these." (Jeremiah 2:34)

1. They were charged with their blood and were rejected by God. (Jeremiah 2:32-37)
2. The Jews pleaded that they lived a clean life and were living morally. (Jeremiah 2:35)
3. God rejected this argument and told them they were guilty by asking the question, "...hast thou also taught the wicked ones they ways?" (Jeremiah 2:33) (+)

C. DAVID PLEADED WITH GOD TO DELIVER HIM FROM BLOOD GUILTINESS
   1. "Deliver me from bloodguiltiness, O God,..." (Psalms 51:14) (+) He promised that he would go back to soul-winning if God would honor his request (Psalms 51:13) But David died with the blood of innocent people on his hands. In II Samuel 18:33, David mourns over his son, Absalom, who died and went to Hell. David continues to mourn in II Samuel 19 and for the rest of his life because he had the blood of his own son on his hands. David was comforted when his infant son died by the knowledge that "I can go where he is [Heaven], but wept uncontrollably when Absalom went to Hell.

D. THEIR LIVES PROVED THEY FELT THEIR RESPONSIBILITY TO THE LOST (+)

Lesson Four

1. Paul persuaded men – He knew the terror of the Lord, we persuaded them. (I Cor. 5:11) "...[He became] all things to all men, that I might by all means SAVE SOME." (I Cor. 9:22)
2. Jude pulled (snatched) them out of the fire (Hell). (Jude 23)
3. Jesus said, "...compel them to come in,..." (Luke 14:23)
4. The early disciples fasted and prayed night and day because they wanted to fulfill their responsibility to the Commission and to the lost. (+)
5. We are commanded to go!
   a. If you go... you will be rewarded
   b. If you ignore the command and do not go... then you will have blood on your hands.

E. ARE YOU JUDGING YOURSELF BY COMPARING YOURSELF TO OTHERS OR BY THE BIBLE?
1. Although Paul warned the believer not to compare themselves with other friends and Christians who lived around them, most of us still do it. In comparing ourselves to others, we believe that if we are doing as well or better than those around us, we will make out pretty well at the Judgment Seat of Christ.
2. God deals with this comparison in the book of James where He informs the believer what to expect when they, as

individuals, stand before the Lord and have their lives and works judged.

3. Each of us would be wise if we memorize the verse that gives this clear distinction. It states, "For he shall have judgment without mercy, that hath shewed no mercy; and mercy rejoiceth against judgment." (James 2:13)

4. **Note** the clear warning, "He [God] shall have judgment without mercy, THAT SHOWED NO MERCY." This meant that when a believer, who lives among sinners who are bound to spend eternity in Hell and shows no mercy by attempting to get them saved, he will receive no mercy from God when he stands before Him at the Judgment Seat. The believer who was self-centered while living his life and had no mercy toward the lost world will find an angry Judge who will severely judge the self-centered believer.

5. But God is quick to add, "and mercy rejoiceth against judgment." This means that the believer who obeys the Commission, "as my Father hath sent me, even so send I you," and has given his life to helping sinners get saved will have a good day and rejoice when he stands at the Judgment Seat of Christ.

6. **One reaps what he sows** – Sow obedience and show mercy toward the lost and dying people and reap mercy

when you stand before God – But oh! Those who do not sow mercy ----- **will receive no mercy!**
F. WHAT IF?
1. What if Jesus **had not** died on the Cross? Your answer, "We would be hopelessly lost in sin, condemned to Hell."
2. What if you will not die to self and accept your personal responsibility to the lost?

FRIDAY

SUMMARY: The Bible stresses method as much as it teaches doctrine. (+) Christianity is not a philosophy. (+) Christianity is a way of life. The Great Commission, according to John, speaks not to people in general, but to the individual in particular. (+) He edifies the believer's job as he tells him that he has power to either remit or retain sin. (+)

A question to each heart, "Do you accept the Great Commission as a philosophy or as a pattern for you to follow, as a way of life?" (+)

Procedure of obtaining and retaining the most from this lesson:

Monday -Read the entire lesson through and then fill-in the blanks for Monday. Do prayer time and daily declarations.
Tuesday - Re-read the material for Tuesday and

fill in the blanks. Review the questions and blanks for Monday. Do prayer time and daily declarations.
Wednesday -Do same – review blanks for Monday and Tuesday. Do prayer time and daily declarations.
Thursday -Do same – review for Monday, Tuesday, and Wednesday. Do prayer time and daily declarations.
Friday - Do same – review for Monday, Tuesday, Wednesday, and Thursday. Do prayer time and daily declarations.

*Read an article one time and retain 6% in two weeks, read for six consecutive days and retain 62%.

Lesson Four   87

MONDAY – THE LESSON'S PURPOSE

1. The _____ in John's account of the Great Commission is on the _____ _____ of the _____ _____.

2. There seems to be very few believers who comprehend the _____ of their _____ responsibility to a lost world.

3. As the Son of God, Jesus _____ the tremendous _____ of the lost.

4. He passed this _____ responsibility on to the _____.

5. Take the responsibility of the believer out of the general _____ and make the _____ _____ believer feel his _____ to the lost world in _____.

TUESDAY – VIVID PRESENTATION

1. Summed up in the _____, "WHAT WOULD JESUS _____?

2. My job on earth is the same _____ God the Father gave His Son to do while _____ was on the _____.

3. "For the Son of Man is come to _____ and to _____ that which was lost."

4. The Great Commission simply bypasses laws, _____, technicalities, and speaks directly to the _____ heart.

5. We need to _____ to _____ and present our body as a living _____.

Lesson Four 89

WEDNESDAY – VIVID POSTSCRIPT

1. I will give some to _____. I believe if I do that, then God _____.

2. I do pray for _____ , when I remember.

3. The postscript to the Great Commission teaches that _____ has power to _____ sins.

4. If the believer _____ to go – if he _____ to pray…then the sinner's sins are retained.

5. This postscript _____ the believer what his responsibility toward the _____ really is.

THURSDAY – VIVID INTERPRETATION

1. Paul was _____ from the _____ of all men. (Acts 20:26-27)

2. "Hast thou also _____ the wicked ones thy _____? (Jeremiah 2:33)

3. "Deliver me from _____, O God." (Psalms 51:14)

4. Their _____ proved they felt their _____ to the lost

5. The _____ disciples fasted and _____ night and _____, because

   they wanted to fulfill their _____ to the _____ and to the _____.

Lesson Four 91

FRIDAY – SUMMARY

1. The Bible _____ method as much as it _____ doctrine.

2. Christianity is not a _____.

3. The Great Commission, according to John, speaks not to people in _____, but to the

   _____ in particular.

4. He edifies the believer's _____ as he tells him that he has power to either _____ or _____ sin.

5. A question to each _____. "Do you accept the Great Commission as a _____?"

DAILY DECLARATION

I do accept my personal responsibility to keep people out of Hell by striving to learn how to become a better witness.

MEMORY VERSE

"For he shall have judgment without mercy, that hath shewed no mercy; and mercy rejoiceth against judgment." (James 2:13)

Check Box after Repeating

Monday	Tuesday	Wednesday	Thursday	Friday

MY COMMITMENT

I accept my personal responsibility and will strive to show mercy toward my fellow man by witnessing to them. I know if I show mercy to people now, God will have mercy on me at the Judgment Seat.

Name_____

Date _____

LESSON FIVE

THE GREAT COMMISSION IN POWER

"But ye shall receive power, after that the Holy Ghost is come upon you: and ye shall be witnesses unto me both in Jerusalem, and in all Judaea, and in Samaria, and unto the uttermost part of the earth." (Acts 1:8)

The Lesson's Outline

I. THE NEED OF POWER TODAY
  A. Is the Great Commission in effect today?
  B. Does this generation need Acts 1:8?
  C. Was the fulfillment of Acts 1:8 the turning point in the early church?

II. THE SOURCE OF POWER TODAY
  A. Dumber than a donkey
    1. It is not in personality
    2. It is not in education
    3. It is not in entertainment
    4. It is not in a system
    5. It is not in facilities
    6. It is not in emotional enthusiasm
  B. From whence cometh Power?
    1. David, the King said
    2. Zachariah, the Priest said
    3. Micah, the Prophet said
    4. Paul, the Apostle said
    5. Jesus, the final authority said

III. THE OBTAINMENT OF POWER TODAY
    A. A desire to have this power
    B. An emptiness of self
    C. An earnest prayer for power
    D. An acceptance by faith
    E. Elisha was a perfect example

THE LESSON'S PURPOSE

The stress in the Book of Acts' account of the Great Commission is on the Power of God. The magnitude of the Church's job would be overwhelming, unless Jesus went with and empower each disciple through the person of the Holy Spirit.

THE LESSON'S MEMORY VERSE
Ephesians 5:18

THE GREAT COMMISSION IN POWER
(Acts 1:8)

Lesson Five

MONDAY

INTRODUCTION: God calls on Dr. Luke to give the final emphasis to the Great Commission in Acts 1:8. (+) Matthew outlined the age-long pattern of making, baptizing, and developing disciples (+) in Matthew 28:18-20. Mark adds to the scope by saying "every creature" in the whole world (+) in Mark 16:15. This will take every individual believer doing Personal Witnessing to accomplish. Luke stressed the message along with the need for the endowment with power (+) in his presentation of the Great Commission in Luke 24:46-49. John clarified the believer's job and places upon him a fearful responsibility to the lost (+) in John 20:21-23

Without this added instruction found in the Great Commission in the Book of Acts, the believer would be overwhelmed. Rethink the situation! The disciples were charged by Jesus to find and preach to every man, woman, boy, and girl in every nation, country, county, city, town, village, and place in the world. If they didn't GO, then those people's sins would be retained. If they did GO, then the people had a chance of their sins being remitted. THIS RESPONSIBILITY WAS OVERWHELMING! IT WAS CRUSHING! The very vastness of the task would discourage and defeat the disciples. THEY NEEDED SOMETHING MORE! They needed the final assurance of God's help and power, which would enable them to be obedient to the command of preaching the Gospel to every creature. They needed the assurance, and God gave it to them by telling them that they would receive power from the Holy Ghost. It would be this power that would allow them to be the powerful witness, God wanted them to be.

TUESDAY

I. THE NEED OF POWER TODAY
   A. IS THE GREAT COMMISSION STILL IN EFFECT? (+) IN ORDER TO DETERMINE THE ANSWER TO THIS QUESTION, CONSIDER THE FOLLOWING:
1. Matthew said, "...unto the end of the world..." or age. (Matthew 28:20)
2. Mark said, "...preach...to every creature." which would include every creature of this generation. (Mark 16:15)
3. Luke said, "...beginning at Jerusalem." And continue among all nations. (Luke 24:47) There is no quitting place.
4. John said, God sent Jesus and Jesus sent us. (John 20:21) If we don't go, then our generation's sin will be retained and we will be held accountable.
5. Luke, in the Book of Acts adds, "Unto the uttermost parts of the world." Our city is the "uttermost" from Jerusalem. It is clear that Jesus gave the Commission and that the command to preach the Gospel to every creature is still in effect and binding upon the disciples today. (+)

B. THIS GENERATION NEEDS ACTS 1:8. This generation manifests the same symptoms that the early Apostles did before they came to Acts 1:8. (+)
   1. The task is too great. There are over seven billion people on the earth today. Oh, the magnitude of the task...EVERY CREATURE!
   2. "I go a fishing." Peter tried to escape and ignore this tremendous task by going fishing. This generation of disciples is also going; they are going fishing, boating, to socials. They are playing church and going everywhere else...as they try to hide from this awesome responsibility of preaching the Gospel to every creature.
   3. Behind closed doors – Before Acts 1:8, the disciples were fearfully hiding behind closed doors. Today's crop of disciples is gathered behind closed doors. They study the "signs," the last day symptoms and the doctrines. Behind closed doors, they listen to the "Word," or they fellowship in their youth groups, ladies' circles, men's brotherhoods, or even their preacher's fellowships.
C. THE FULFILLMENT OF ACTS 1:8 WAS THE TURNING POINT. (+) They were filled with the Holy Spirit. (Acts 2:4)
   1. They were no longer overwhelmed by the tremendous task. They took to the streets and had...

a. 3,000 saved and baptized on the day of Pentecost (Acts 2:41)
   b. Daily additions thereafter (Acts 2:47)
   c. 5,000 men saved (Acts 4:4)
   d. Multitudes, both men and women (Acts 5:14)
   e. Then they began to be multiplied (Acts 6:1)
   f. Finally, they were multiplied greatly. (Acts 6:7) This continued until the whole city was evangelized. The historians say that well over 100,000 were converted. Their critics charge them with, "Filling the whole city with your doctrine." (Acts 5:28) Soon the church in Jerusalem became churches in Judea, Galilee, and Samaria and was multiplied in number. (Acts 9:31) This started a missionary movement that swept the whole world as they evangelized their generation in their day. (Col. 1:23)
2. It could happen in our day. The excitement, the joy, the success that the early churches and disciples experienced can HAPPEN IN OUR DAY ALSO! There are basically three thing which must happen:
   a. We must accept the Great Commission literally as our working orders.

b. We must return to the New Testament method of training and developing converts.
c. We must be EMPOWERED! If the need of divine poser was so great in the New Testament days, how much more is this power needed today? Spurgeon said, "A church should close her doors rather than be without the divine power of the Holy Spirit." With the world on the brink of disaster, with sin gripping the world like a huge steel vice, with lukewarmness and heresy paralyzing the Christian world, how can anyone fail to see where the modern church is failing? It has everything the successful churches of the past had, except the most important element...POWER. (+)

WEDNESDAY

II. THE SOURCE OF POWER TODAY. IF THE NEED OF POWER IS SO GREAT, THEN WHERE CAN ONE OBTAIN THIS LIFE SAVING QUALITY? WHAT IS THE SOURCE OF THIS POWER?

A. DUMBER THAN A DONKEY. God, by the mouth of Isaiah, spoke these words in Isaiah 1:3, "The ox knoweth his owner, and the ass his master's crib: but Israel doth not know, my people doth not consider." God said that many dumb animals had better sense than His own chosen people. (+) This is true today. Many people have less intelligence than a donkey when it comes to knowing where and how to obtain this great power.

1. IT IS NOT IN PERSONALITY. A good personality is a wonderful asset and blessing from God and is to be highly prized. But if one depends on personality alone for his power to win, he is doomed to defeat! God's power is not in a good personality. (+)
2. IT IS NOT IN EDUCATION. If a Christian is a "hick," he will fail! But it would be better to be a "hick" with power than a highly-educated believer with no power. God needs a man with power and training. How sad it is to see that most have missed this point. They want to be accepted as church members of dignity and polish, but **display little concern for real power with God.** Power is not in education.
3. IT IS NOT IN ENTERTAINMENT. Many churches have tried to hold their crowd by entertaining them. Hence, they have become nothing more than a social club. They have compromised their beliefs and made their grandchildren atheists. Woe unto the people who try to succeed through entertainment! There is no power from this source!

4. IT IS NOT IN A SYSTEM. Many personal workers depend on a system to obtain needed power and win souls. A system does not have power, regardless of how good or how appealing it may be! (+)
5. IT IS NOT IN FACILITIES. Buildings, classrooms, choir lofts, pews, or everything desirable in the field of facilities is not power. The spiritual condition of most churches has **suffered greatly following a successful building program.** There is no power in facilities, regardless of how beautiful and appealing they may appear.
6. IT IS NOT EMOTIONAL ENTHUSIASM. Enthusiasm is wonderful. Without some enthusiasm it is very difficult to win people, but if a person depends upon emotional means he will never have the real power of God in his life. He will have a cheap imitation, **which will eventually cause him to become defeated**, for power is not in emotional enthusiasm.

B. FROM WHENCE COMETH POWER? If power is not found in the physical realm, and if there is nothing the fleshly graces can do to produce the power that will bring success, then from whence cometh this power? (+)
1. DAVID, THE KING, SAID, "God hath spoken once; twice have I heard this;

that **power belongeth unto God**." (Psalms 62:11)
2. ZECHARIAH, THE PRIEST, SAID, "...Not by might, nor by power, **but by my spirit, saith the LORD of hosts.**" (Zachariah 4:6)
3. MICAH, THE PROPHET, SAID, "But truly I am full of power by the spirit of the LORD,..." (Micah 3:8)
4. PAUL, THE GREAT APOSTLE, SAID, "...be strong in the Lord, and in the power of His might." **(+)** (Ephesians 6:10) "(For the weapons of our warfare are not carnal, but mighty through God to the pulling down of strong holds;)..." (II Corinthians 10:4) "And be not drunk with wine, wherein is excess; but be filled with the Spirit;" (Ephesians 5:18) "Quench not the Spirit." (I Thessalonians 5:19)
5. JESUS CHRIST, THE FINAL AUTHORITY, SAID, "But ye shall receive power, after that the Holy Ghost is come upon you:..." (Acts 1:8) "...but tarry ye in the city of Jerusalem, until ye be endued with power from on high." (Luke 24:49) "...how much more shall your heavenly Father give the Holy Spirit to them that ask him?" (Luke 11:13)

THURSDAY

III. THE OBTAINMENT OF POWER TODAY

If the empowerment, which comes from the Holy Spirit is so vital...if it is the difference between success and failure... (+) if it is the difference between "hanging on out of duty" and having the exciting, happy life described as "joy unspeakable and full of glory." HOW DOES ONE OBTAIN THIS POWER? (+) Consider the following principles:

  A. A DESIRE TO HAVE THIS POWER
  1. The thirsty shall be filled. We use the word "desire," which does not adequately describe the intensity of the desire. We should desire the power of God as a thirsty man craves a drink of water. (+)
  2. The promise! "Blessed...for [the thirsty] shall be filled." (Matthew 5:6)

  B. AN EMPTINESS OF SELF
  1. One can't fill a full vessel! There isn't any way one can fill a container that is already full. (+)
  2. Full of world. Many twentieth century Christians walk like the world, talk like the world, dress like the world, and live in the world! They become enemies of God. (Philippians 3:8; James 4:4) We must come out of the world and be separate, and then we can claim His promise in II Corinthians 6:17-18.

3. Full of self. Many are so concerned about being noticed and receiving credit, that God can't use them. **(+)** WE need to die to self (Romans 6:11) and present our bodies a living sacrifice. (Romans 12:1)

C. AN EARNEST PRAYER FOR POWER
1. A good example. In Luke 11:13, Jesus said, "If ye then, being evil, know how to give good gifts…." Jesus is comparing that just as parents love to give a nice gift to their children God loves to give to his children.
2. How much more…if you like to give good gifts to your children…how much more does our Heavenly Father like to give to His children?
3. His choice gift. He gives the Holy Spirit to those who ASK Him. **(+)** (Luke 11:13) "…ye have not, because ye ask not." (James 4:2)
4. Ask and ye shall receive. (Matthew 7:7)

D. AN OBEDIENCE TO THE SCRIPTURES
1. The promise of God, "…so is also the Holy Ghost, whom God hath given to them that OBEY HIM." (Acts 5:32)

FRIDAY

E. AN ACCEPTANCE BY FAITH
1. After you have a desire to be filled and empowered by God.
2. After you have turned from the world and selfish desires.
3. After you have prayed for power and for the filling of the Spirit.
4. After you have obeyed the Scriptures. (+)
5. Then, ACCEPT GOD at His Word and allow Him to use and empower you. (+) "...Receive ye the Spirit...by the hearing of faith?" Galatians 3:2-5; Galatians 5:25)
6. Elisha is a perfect example. Elisha was a young preacher who wanted to have the power of God in his life. He thirsted for the power of God. Followed Elijah around for days because he wanted a double portion of Elijah's power with God. He gave up farming and the things of the world in order to obtain Gods power. He was evidently praying for this power as he went from place to place following Elijah. He was obeying Elijah [Word of God] as he was told – if you see me leave for Heaven, then your prayers will be answered for the power of God in your life. He showed that exercising faith in obtaining the power of God [being filled by the Holy Spirit]

was not belief alone, but by obeying God through taking action. Elisha showed his faith that he was filled with the Holy Spirit by taking Elijah's mantel and striking the waters which parted. Faith without works is dead. Elisha demonstrated his faith that he had been filled with God's power by striking the water. This is where many of God's preachers and children fail to obtain the filling of the Spirit today. They do all that the Bible teaches they should do, except act upon the promise, which God has promised them. **They wait for a feeling and do not act.** When they do not act upon God's promise, they manifest unbelief. They continue in their powerless life because their faith is dead without claiming God's promise and acting upon it.

SUMMARY: The Word of God teaches method as well as doctrine. (+) God's method of making disciples is through the empowering of the Holy Spirit. (+) When we return to the New Testament method of training and developing our new converts and learn to depend on the Holy Spirit to give us genuine conversion, the WE WILL ALSO RETURN TO THE NEW TESTAMENT RESULTS AND FRUITFULNESS. (+)

Procedure of obtaining and retaining the most from this lesson:

Monday -Read the entire lesson through and then fill-in the blanks for Monday. Do prayer time and daily declarations.

Tuesday - Re-read the material for Tuesday and fill in the blanks. Review the questions and blanks for Monday. Do prayer time and daily declarations.

Wednesday -Do same – review blanks for Monday and Tuesday. Do prayer time and daily declarations.

Thursday - Do same – review for Monday, Tuesday, and Wednesday. Do prayer time and daily declarations.

Friday - Do same – review for Monday, Tuesday, Wednesday, and Thursday. Do prayer time and daily declarations.

*Read an article one time and retain 6% in two weeks, read for six consecutive days and retain 62%.

MONDAY – THE GREAT COMMISSION

1. God calls on Dr. _____ to give the final _____ to the Great Commission in _____.

2. _____ outlined the _____ long pattern of making, baptizing, and developing disciples.

3. _____ adds the scope by saying, "_____ creature" in the _____ world.

4. _____ stressed the _____ along with the need for the endowment with _____.

5. _____ clarified the believer's job and places upon him a fearful _____ to the lost.

Lesson Five

TUESDAY – THE NEED

1. Is the Great Commission _____ in effect?

2. The _____ to preach the Gospel to every creature is _____ in _____ and _____ upon the

   disciples today.

3. This _____ manifest the same symptoms that the early _____ did before they came to _____.

4. The fulfillment of _____ was the turning point.

5. It has _____ the successful churches of the past had, except the most _____ element _____.

WEDNESDAY – THE SOURCE

1. God said that many dumb _____ had better sense than his chosen _____.

2. God's power is not in a _____ personality.

3. A system does _____ have power regardless of how _____ or how _____ it may be!

4. If power is not found in the _____ realm, and if there is _____ the fleshly _____ can

   do to produce the power that will bring success, then from whence cometh this _____?

5. "…be strong in the _____, and in the _____ of his might."

Lesson Five

THURSDAY – THE OBTAINMENT

1. If it is the _____ between success and failure, how does one _____ this power?

2. We should desire the power of God as a _____ man _____ a drink of water.

3. There isn't any way one can _____ a container that is already _____.

4. Many are so concerned about being _____ and receiving _____, that God cannot use _____.

5. He gives the Holy Spirit to those who _____ Him.

FRIDAY – AN ACCEPTANCE – SUMMARY

1. After you have _____ the scriptures.

2. Then, accept God at His Word and allow Him to _____ and _____ you.

3. The Word of God teaches _____ as well as doctrine.

4. God's method of making _____ is through the _____ of the Holy Spirit.

5. When we return to the New _____ method of training…WE WILL ALSO RETURN

   TO THE NEW _____ RESULTS AND _____.

Lesson Five

DAILY DECLARATION

I will strive to humble myself and obey the Lord in order for Him to fill me with His power for service.

MEMORY VERSE

"And be not drunk with wine, wherein is excess; but be filled with the Spirit;"
(Ephesians 5:18)

Check Box after Repeating

Monday	Tuesday	Wednesday	Thursday	Friday

MY COMMITMENT

Having studied this lesson on the command, need for, and the method of becoming a spirit-filled Christian, I will humbly submit to and trust God for his empowerment.

Name_____

Date _____

LESSON SIX

YOUR FINANCIAL OBLIGATION TO GIVE UNDER THE GREAT COMMISSION

INTRODUCTION
MONDAY

In Romans 10:13, Paul boldly states the great news that **"For whosoever shall call upon the name of the Lord shall be saved."** (+) As a missionary, he penned the questions which reveal our personal and financial obligation within the Great Commission. (+)

He asked:
- "How then shall they call on him whom they have not believed?"
- "and how shall they believe in him of whom they have not heard?"
- "and how shall they hear without a preacher [messenger]?"
- "And how shall they preach, except they be sent?" (+) Romans 10:14

In this one wonderful statement and four heart searching questions God spotlights the fearful responsibility of **every member of the local church.** (+)

LEARN THIS LESSON EARLY IN LIFE.

As we journey through this life.
From the cradle to the grave.

The part of life one gives
Is the only part **that is saved!** (+)

I. FINANCIAL OBLIGATION VIEWED AS A RESPONSIBILITY

TUESDAY
A. RESPONSIBILITY TO BE SHARED BY ALL

Jesus gave the Great Commission to His church of saved, baptized believers. In order to come to your personal obligation under this age long commission please consider three negatives and one positive declaration.

1. **The Commission wasn't given just to preachers.** (+) Preachers are part of the local body of Christ and as such must bear responsibility of getting the gospel to the lost world. But the commission does not place them under any more responsibility than it does any other saved person.
2. **The Commission wasn't given to just the called.** The Bible teaches that God calls men into the mission field. (Acts 13:1-3). This special call does not supersede the command of Jesus which is found in the Great Commission. It identifies their particular field of labor and purpose, but it does not add more responsibility than what they already had.
3. **The Commission wasn't given to just the gifted.** Many seem to think that if one

has the means then he can give to missions. Somehow, in their thinking, there are levels of responsibility to missions. **Preachers, deacons, and those that can afford to give have a responsibility, but many who are not "gifted" are excused.** This is false thinking *which was* forever dispelled by the story of the widow who gave her mites to the Lord. "...For unto whomsoever much is given, of him shall be much required:..." (Luke 12:48) This is true, but it does not NULLIFY the obligation placed upon all by the Great Commission.

4. **The Commission was given to all members.** In Romans 1:14, Paul stated the personal responsibility of every believer when he wrote; "**I am debtor** both to the **Greeks,** and to the **Barbarians;** both to the **wise,** and to the **unwise.**" We owe them the Gospel!

B. RESPONSIBILITY IS TO BE SHARED EQUALLY

1.**The missionary and his family give all.** (+) They sell their home, give up their treasurers, personal items, say goodbye to loved ones and friends and go to an uncertain place of service. **Much sacrifice and human denial goes into their decision**. Stop and personalize their decision by visualizing the faces of your children or grandchildren on the face, of the next missionary who visits your church. **Missionaries give all!**

2. **The informed give** money. It is amazing at the percentage of money that many in local churches give to the Lord. It seems that the more a person learns about the Bible and by faith follows it's teaching, **the more he abounds in his giving**. But most Christians limit their obedience to the Great Commission by giving money. When they give, it seems that **they feel like** they fulfilled their responsibility to the commission.

3. **The average member gives little.** Many give a waitress a bigger tip than they give to missions. (+)

4. **"But by an equality,..."** The inspired word states that every believer is under the **same obligation.** In his second letter to the Corinthian church, Paul said that God didn't intend for some to be **burdened while others are at ease** (doing nothing) "But by an **equality,...**" (II Cor. 8:13-14) God does not require some to give all, others give money and the rest give nothing. This unscriptural practice causes harm, discouragement and failure in the Lord's work. The Bible teaches an equal responsibility under the Great Commission. **(+)**

C. RESPONSIBILITY TO GIVE PRAYERS, ENCOURAGEMENT AS WELL AS FINANCIAL SUPPORT.

If all of our members gave financial support to missionaries, it would bring revival. Imagine what could happen if we begin to get involved by:

1. **Becoming acquainted with our missionaries.** A church could become acquainted with our missionaries and their families by developing an informational booklet. In **this** booklet we would place the name, age, hobby, and photograph of each member of the **family**. There could be testimonies with other personal information about their backgrounds. A church could have a reception for the **family** where each member of the family was recognized and awarded. Many members testify that they had a life changing experience when a missionary and his family were guests in their home.
2. **Becoming informed.** In addition to special services, the letters of missionaries can be posted on the Mission Board. Portions of letters could be read before Sunday School classes or services.
3. **Becoming involved.** Special prayer meetings could be held regarding missionaries and their needs. Gifts could be donated and sent to missionaries and their families on special occasions. **The focus of the church should be on our business. The**

church's business is Missions. (+) As part of the local church family, it is your obligation to get involved in prayer for, in the encouragement of, as well as in the financial support of our missionaries.

II. FINANCIAL OBLIGATION VIEWED AS AN EXERCISE OF FAITH

WEDNESDAY

A. **COMMANDED TO GROW IN GRACE AND IN KNOWLEDGE.**
The Apostle Peter was the first, and perhaps the most successful pastor God ever chose. It was under his human leadership that the Holy Spirit performed the works recorded in the first eight Chapters of Acts. The last words of this great pastor should be considered as among the most important words found in the Bible. His last words were, "But g**row in grace,** and in the **knowledge** of our Lord and Saviour Jesus Christ...." (II Peter 3:18) **(+)**
    1. **The natural laws of growth.** As soon as a healthy baby is born he begins to grow. This principle is true in the spiritual realm also. **The baby must have both food and exercise** in order to develop into a healthy normal child.
    2. **Notice grace as well as knowledge.** Grace, as used here, **has reference to ability**. The child of God is commanded to grow in his performance as well as in

knowledge. A little child naturally grows in his ability as he becomes older. (+) Once he had to be hand-fed but now he is able to feed himself. Once he was fearful and uncertain but now he has confidence and assurance. **It came through the natural process of growth.**

3. **The grace of giving.** The church at Corinth had a rough beginning, but through the ministry of Paul it grew into one of the greatest churches in the world. In II Corinthians 8:7, Paul is commending them for their spiritual growth and improvements. He told them that **they had grown in every area;** in faith, in utterance, in knowledge, in their love toward him and please take note, **"ye abound in this grace also"** referring to their growth in giving. (+) The verse is teaching the natural process of the growth of a child of God which includes the ability to grow in the ability to give. This means that the child of God can and should grow in the ability to give today.

B. **COMETH BY KNOWLEDGE (Hearing)**
1. **Knowledge of God's procedure.** "...faith cometh by hearing, and hearing by the word of God." (Romans 10:17.) God's procedure of growth in a child of God comes through hearing the Word of God. When a child of God learns the Word of God, it produces a growth within the child of God.

2. **Knowledge of God's promises.** It is marvelous at the transformation which takes place within the being of a new convert as he learns of God's love and promises.
3. **Knowledge of God's provisions.** The promises speaks of God provision for the well-being of his child. When the new convert begins to realize who he is (God's child), what he has (all of God's power and provision), and what he will possess forever, it produces tremendous change and growth in his life.

C. **CONSUMMATED THROUGH EXERCISE.** All the **promises** and provisions which God offers to the child of God are **meaningless** unless they are accepted. One must believe and exercise faith in order to claim the promises. "But without faith it is impossible to please him [God]:..." (Heb. 11:6)

1. **God said, "...prove me...."** In Malachi 3:10, God challenges his people to prove Him! The subject under consideration is tithes and offerings and God is boldly promising to bless them if they will only exercise their faith and obey. This is only one of many such promises which God makes to the believers! These promises are *given* to stimulate one to exercise his faith and accept or do God's will. "...faith, if it hath not works, is dead...." (James 2:17) The emphasis in the Bible is to be a **doer** of the Word, not a hearer only. (James 1:22) **(+)**
2. **God's proven plan.** There may be other good plans to get God's people to give liberally to

Lesson Six 123

God and missions but the one that the writer prefers is called, "Faith Promise." This plan is taken directly from the Bible and if implemented and followed properly will cause the members of the local church to both grow in faith and in giving.

A church sets aside a time in which missionaries come to the church for special services. During that time they stress the promises of God toward those who, by faith, will obey Him. Through the combination of the missionaries helping the people see the needs of their fields, the promises of God's blessing upon those who give; a challenge is made. The challenge is - by faith. Set a certain amount such as $1, $5, $50 per week and as God supplies that amount; give it into the special mission account. **This amount is above the tithe and offering which they are already giving.** As God supplies that amount, they give it.

Many churches, as well as individuals, have been transformed by this "Faith Promise" principle. (+) One grows through knowledge (learning about the need and as well as God's promised provision) and then by faith (exercise) doing it.

III. FINANCIAL OBLIGATION VIEWED AS AN ETERNAL INVESTMENT

THURSDAY
A. MANY GIVE OUT OF HABIT.
1. **It is Sunday -** give. Many have gone to church

so long that it is a routine or habit. May I quickly add, it is a good habit, but still a habit.
2. **It is offering time - give.** Each Sunday the ushers come forward, the musician plays and it is time to give; so they give.
3. **It is need time - give.** It is not unusual in the average church to have some special need arise. The offering plate is passed and people respond by giving. It is the thing to do. So we do it!

B. **MANY GIVE BECAUSE IT IS COMMANDED (+)**
 1. **Command of what?** "Bring ye all the tithes into the storehouse,..." (Mal. 3:10) God commands it and we obey by doing it.
 2. **Command of when?** "Upon the first day of the week let every one of you lay by him in store, as God hath prospered him,..." (I Corinthians 16:2) It is the first day of the week, Sunday, so we obey God's command and give!
 3. **Command of why?** "...to prove the sincerity of your love." (II Corinthians 8:8) The child of God expresses his love to his heavenly father by his obedience in giving.
 4. **Command of where?** The tithe was brought to the storehouse (Mal 3:10) in the Old Testament era and to the local church in the New Testament. Judas was the first Treasurer.

Thank God for the many who give because the Word of God commands it. They know what,

Lesson Six 125

when, why and where to give and they do it. Praise God for these faithful, loving people but the Bible teaches a better way.

C. **MANY GIVE AS AN ETERNAL INVESTMENT.** Many Christians think hard and long about their secular investments. They will seek advice and even pay for special information or counsel, but these same people give very little thought concerning the gifts of their tithes and offerings.

1. **Investment into heaven's bank.** God does have a bank and he commands His people to "...lay up for yourselves treasurers in heaven,..." (Matt. 6:20)
2. **Investments into the lives of others.** The book of Philippians was written by a missionary (Paul) to his sponsoring church which was located in Philippi. There are many tremendous truths presented in this missionary letter. Perhaps, the greatest truth and the one which pertains to our subject is found in Phil. 4:17. Paul speaks about the many offerings which the church gave him. He clarified why he was so grateful for their support and offerings. He said, "Not because I desire a gift [money]; but I desire fruit [results] that may abound to your account." Paul is telling them that the support they sent time and again was more than a gift; **it was an investment in his ministry.** Their gift was a gift but it was much more than a gift. **It was an investment.** In a **manner** of speaking they had bought **shares in**

his missionary activities and souls won in the city of Phillipi. They would share in the results of that great church's ministry. They would share in the results of all the ministries of those who were saved in Phillipi and later started preaching!

"Fruit that may abound to your account". Note two words: Abound and account. (+) Abound speaks of multi-level multiplication while account refers to credit or reward. The people of Phillipi who supported the missionary, Paul, will never realize the vastness and richness of their **investment** until they all stand together at the bank of heaven where the value of their account (shares) will be published.

3. **Investment depends on one's sowing (giving).** The Bible teaches that one will reap what he sows. If one sows bountifully then he will reap a large or bountiful harvest. (+)

In many companies they have a payroll deductible pension plan. Each employee determines if he wants to participate in the plan and the amount he wishes to have withheld from his check. Many have tremendous retirement plans and enjoy great freedom and luxury because they invested a small amount each week which grew into a great fund through the compound interest it earned.

Why don't you lay up for yourself treasurers in heaven. Learn to consider your giving as an **investment.** Some could begin to invest $20 a week. Others may be able to invest $50 per week. Drive

Lesson Six

that old car for another year and invest (the difference between a higher car payment and your present payment) in the <u>ministry</u> of your church and missionaries. You would live just as well now, but oh the <u>difference</u> you would enjoy during the 1000 year reign of Christ. (+) What fruit would abound to your account --- compound interest and you would enjoy that investment **forever.**

4. **Investment which pays compound interest.** Today, the best retirement plan will cease to be the investor's **and go to another upon the investor's death.** Someone's sacrifice and careful planning is voided by death. The person will receive no personal benefit from all his planning and effort, but **God has a plan which far exceeds the best retirement plans** which was ever developed by man.

CONSIDER GOD'S SUPER-DUPER PLAN

In the last book of the Bible a representative of the bank of heaven begins to make an announcement of God's **Super Duper Investment Plan.** In the midst of his announcement concerning the plan of all plans for investors, the excited author of the plan burst through the announcement by shouting a gigantic, "YESSSS!" All of heaven stares in amazement as the Holy Spirit finishes the unbelievable announcement of benefits. "...that they [investors who died] may rest from their labours; and their WORKS DO FOLLOW them." (Rev. 14:13) (+)

God's dear children, who had followed him by faith and invested their lives and monies in the work of God, died! Their lives ended! Their personal giving, praying, witnessing and working ended. They died! Their physical walk among men on this earth ceased.

They followed in the steps of Stephen who cried out, "...Lord Jesus, receive my spirit," (Acts 7:59) and then went to heaven.

In Rev. 14:13, the angel declares that some of the saved died. He states their race on the earth was over. Their physical service to Christ was through. There will be no more tears, no more prayers, no more heartaches, no more persecution! They are at peace. They are resting.

It was at this point that the Holy Spirit shouted out, "YES." But look at those benefits. Look at those investments, which they made in the lives and **ministries** of other. Look at that compound interest. It is doubling, Quadrupling... Multiplying... **Multiplying**... MULTIPLYING. Their investments paid dividends while they were **alive**, but it is paying greater dividends after they died. **"...their works do follow them." (Revelation 14:13)**

SUMMARY:

It is good to be obedient and give. (+) God will bless you for it. **But when you learn to consider your giving as investments, it is at this point when the real joy and excitement begins.**

Notice some of the improvements in service this new knowledge will bring:

1) One will take better care of God's facilities-- Why? Because it is **part of his investment.**
2) One **will pray** more earnestly for the missionary. Why? Because the missionary **is a co-worker** who is **steward over one of your investments.** (+)
3) One will assist and help people more and become a greater servant. Why? Their **personal investment** is at stake; they are investing in something or service in that person's life. This understanding causes one to become responsible.
4) It is God's way for me **to lay up treasure** in heaven by helping others. (+)
5) It is God's way for me to **glorify Christ** by bearing more fruit. "Herein is my Father glorified, that ye bear much fruit;..." (John 15:8) (+)

CONCLUSION
LEARN THIS LESSON EARLY IN LIFE

As we journey through life

From the cradle to the grave

The part of your life you give

Is the ONLY PART that you save. (+)

Introduction
Monday

1. _____ shall call upon the name of the Lord shall be_____

2. He penned the_____ which reveal our _____ financial obligation within the Great Commission.

3. How shall they_____ except they be_____?

4. God spotlights the fearful responsibility of _____ member of the local church.

5. The part of life one_____ is the part that is_____.

Lesson Six

As a Responsibility
Tuesday

1. The commission wasn't given just to_____.

2. The missionary and his _____give all.

3. Many give a waitress a bigger _____than they give to _____.

4. The_____ teaches an _____responsibility under the Great Commission.

5. The focus of the church should be on our_____. The Church's _____ is Missions.

As an Exercise of Faith
Wednesday

1. But grow in _____ and in the knowledge of our _____ Jesus Christ.

2. A _____ child naturally grows in his _____ as he becomes older.

3. "Ye abound in this _____ also" referring to their growth in _____

4. The emphasis in the _____ is to be a _____ of the Word.

5. Many _____, as well as individuals, have been transformed by this _____ principle.

Lesson Six   133

As an Investment
Thursday

1. Many _____ because it is commanded.

2. Fruit that may _____ to your account. Note two words: _____ and _____.

3. If one sows _____ then he will reap a_____ or_____ harvest.

4. You would live just as_____ now but oh the_____ you would enjoy during the _____ year reign.

5. That they [investor's who have_____] may rest from their _____; and their works do _____ them"

Summary
Friday

1. It is good to be _____ and _____.

2. Because the _____ is a _____ who is _____ over one of your investments.

3. It is God's way for me to _____ up treasures in _____ by helping others.

4. "Herein is my _____ glorified that _____ bear much _____;…"

5. The part of your life you _____ is the only part that you _____

Lesson Six

DAILY DECLARATION

I will strive to lay up treasures by investing in other ministries while I am on earth.

MEMORY VERSE

"Lay not up for yourselves treasures upon earth, where moth and rust doth corrupt, and where thieves break through and steal: But lay up for yourselves treasures in heaven, where neither moth nor rust doth corrupt, and where thieves do not break through nor steal:"
(Matthew 6:19-20)

CHECK BLOCK AFTER REPEATING

	Mon	Tues	Wed	Thurs	Fri	Sat	Sun
A.M.							
P.M.							

MY COMMITMENT

Having studied that giving is an investment which pays eternal dividends while getting people saved from hell, I make a commitment to do my best.

NAME:_____ GRADE_____

YAKIMA BIBLE BAPTIST CHURCH
6201 TIETON DRIVE
YAKIMA, WA. 98908
509-966-1912